D1518561

AN AWESOME
BIBLE STORIES
ADVENTURE

Abraham's family

Edited by John D. Morris

Original text : Albert Hari, Charles Singer
English text : Caroline Morson

Illustrations : Mariano Valsesia, Betti Ferrero

**Great Oaks
Children's Library**

CHAPTER 1

Abraham's departure

Marc Chagall
(1887-1985),
Abraham and
the three Angels,
oil on hard canvas.

© Photo R.M.N. - Gérard Blot / A.D.A.G.P. / Musée du Message biblique, Nice (France)

Departure

Nomad in the Libyan desert

Near the town of Ur (whose ruins are situated in today's Iraq) a tribe of nomadic shepherds broke camp. The tent pegs were pulled out, and the great black cloths folded. All the possessions were loaded onto donkeys, and the caravan set off. It left the huge city of Ur with all its temples and false gods.

We can only wonder why Terah and his family decided to leave their comfortable hometown of Ur, for the Bible doesn't tell. Evidently Terah believed in God, for he had been entrusted with records of the creation and flood, which were later passed on to his son, Abraham. Did Terah feel the call of God to leave the idolotrous city of Ur? Were he and Abraham both on a mission to start a new nation which honored God? If so, Terah didn't finish his journey, for he settled in the region of Haran instead (in the southern part of today's country of Turkey). Soon God called Abraham to leave his father and journey on to the land of Canaan*, the "promised land."

Donkey loaded with provisions

Abraham's faith

Details of the lives of Abraham and his descendants were recorded on scrolls or tablets. They passed down through the generations, and eventually were given to Moses, who put them together into the book we now call Genesis. It emphasizes several important aspects of Abraham's life and faith:

1. Abraham's departure was not just the beginning of a migration. It was a response in obedience to God's call.
2. Abraham is depicted as the first true believer. He left his country and its idols in order to follow the one true God.
3. In Abraham's call the whole of the history of humanity is already contained in embryonic form. All the peoples of the earth are blessed in him.

* The Land of Canaan
Abraham lived around 2000 B.C. Both the Bible and archaeological discoveries tell us that the people of Canaan were wicked and worshiped idols. But Abraham was a man of great faith, and continued to worship God. God blessed him greatly.

God said

Genesis Chapter 12; 1-7.

Now the Lord had said unto **Abram**, *Get thee out of thy country, and from thy kindred, and from thy father's house, unto a land that I will shew thee : And I will make of thee a great nation, and I will bless thee, and make thy name great; and thou shalt be a **blessing** : And I will bless them that bless thee, and curse him that curseth thee : and in thee shall all families of the earth be blessed.*

So Abram departed, as the Lord had spoken unto him; and Lot went with him : and Abram was seventy and five years old when he departed out of Haran. And Abram took Sarai his wife, and Lot his brother's son, and all their substance that they had gathered, and the souls that they had gotten in Haran; and they went forth to go into the land of **Canaan** ; and into the land of Canaan they came.

And Abram passed through the land unto the place of Sichem, unto the plain of Moreh. And the Canaanite was then in the land. And the Lord appeared unto Abram, and said, Unto thy seed will I give this land: and there builded he an altar unto the Lord, who appeared unto him.

Abram and Abraham

Why does this text speak of Abram and not of Abraham ? When the time was right, God was to change the name of His servant. Abram (which means "exalted father") became Abraham (which means "father of a multitude"). He was to be the human father of many nations, including the people of Israel, and the spiritual father of all who believed in the true God.

Blessing

God blessed Abraham. This meant that he wanted to make him happy, him, his family and all humanity. In the Bible, joy, peace, friendship and prosperity are seen as a blessing.

Canaan

This was the country where Jesus was to live many years later. Over the centuries, many nations have ruled this land. Today it consists mainly of Israel.

5

God is close

God speaks

God desires a loving relationship with every man or woman, boy or girl. Even though people are very different from God, He makes Himself known to us in various ways. He loves us, like a father loves his beloved children.

The Bible

Today we have God's word, the Bible, to tell us what He is like and what he has done for us. It tells us of His love and of our responsibility to obey Him, and how we can be *"born again"* into His family.

God calls

God calls each of His children to follow Him and His commandments. Sometimes, like He did with Abraham, He calls a person to a special job. If we love Him more than anything else and love our friends and neighbors also, we will please our heavenly Father.

Departure

Hearing the call of God and choosing to be faithful to Him is like a departure on a long journey! It consists of making progress, despite the obstacles, on the path which leads us day by day to please Him more, and to be more loving to our neighbors.

Blessing

God blesses all the people in the world. He gives life and breath, rain and sunshine. He gives them rules by which to live and be satisfied. But most of all, He gave us His son as a gift of His love. Through His son, Jesus Christ, we can enjoy God's fullest blessings in this life, and a close relationship with Him, in heaven, for all eternity.

Difficult departure

Departure
on a long journey
to which God calls us
can fill us with fear.

Which are the paths
we will tread
and where will they lead?
Perhaps there will be
a turning to be taken
which I would rather avoid?

And perhaps
I will even have to change
my behavior,
thinking of others first
and starting to share?

Setting out is not difficult
when we have firmly rooted
in our hearts
the trust which knows
that whatever happens
God is present
as a companion
throughout the long journey!

CHAPTER • 2

A long road

Horace Vernet (1789-1863),
Hagar sent away by Abraham (1837)
detail, oil on canvas.

© Giraudon - Musée des Beaux-Arts, Nantes (France)

A great traveler

Children on a donkey

In the time of Abraham the breeders of small livestock (sheep and goats) often moved around in search of pasture. They traveled the hills and valleys, on the borders of the desert, where they could find water-holes for the flocks.

Abraham was a great traveler. He traveled the whole fertile Crescent: from Ur (in Mesopotamia), through the land of Haran (in Turkey), to Canaan, the Negev (the desert), and Egypt, finally returning to settle in Canaan. All along the way he bore in his heart the twofold desire of the nomad: numerous descendants and, one day, owning land*.

A twofold promise

The Bible does not speak of Abraham's desires, but of God's promises: the promise of descendants and of land. Yet both were a long time in coming. An overview of Abraham's life shows us that the life of even a faithful follower of God can be an uphill climb. Abraham had left his country. When he arrived in the land of Canaan, God promised it to him. But there was disappointment as a great drought struck, and Abraham left for Egypt. There Pharaoh took his wife, but he got her back and returned to Canaan. Then he let his nephew Lot settle in the greenest part of the land, the fertile valley of the Jordan River. Abraham was left with the arid mountains. God had promised him descendants. Was this possible? Abraham's wife was barren. What did it matter? According to the customs of the time he had a son with his servant Hagar: *Ishmael***. Would he be the heir? Then God intervened and Sarah had a son in her old age, just as God had promised: *Isaac*. Everything was in the balance again until God asked Abraham to sacrifice his son. Faithful Abraham obeyed, but at the last moment God provided a ram as a substitute sacrifice for Isaac. Abraham's son was to live. It was only toward the end of his life that Abraham officially acquired the first fragment of the promised land, when he bought a field in which to bury his wife. God fulfills His promises, but not always as we except Him to.

The camel: the ship of the desert

* During his long journey Abraham and his tribe traveled through the countries which are now known as: Iraq, Syria, Turkey, Lebanon, Israel and Egypt.
See the map on page 35.

** See page 11: **Ishmaël.**

Count the stars

Genesis Chapter 12 : 10 ; Chapter 13 : 1, 12, 14, 15 ; Chapter 15 : 5 ; Chapter 21 : 2, 3, 6.

And there was a famine in the land : and Abram went down into Egypt to sojourn there ; for the famine was grievous in the land. And Abram went up out of Egypt, he, and his wife, and all that he had, and Lot with him, into the south. Abram dwelled in the land of Canaan, and Lot dwelled in the cities of the plain, and pitched his tent toward Sodom.

And the Lord said unto Abram, after that Lot was separated from him, *Lift up now thine eyes, and look from the place where thou art northward, and southward, and eastward, and westward : For all the land which thou seest, to thee will I give it, and to thy seed for ever.* And he brought him forth abroad, and said, *Look now toward heaven, and tell the stars, if thou be able to number them :* and he said unto him, *So shall thy seed be.* For Sarah conceived, and bare Abraham a son in his old age, at the set time of which God had spoken to him. And Abraham called the name of his son that was born unto him, whom Sarah bare to him, **Isaac**. And Sarah said, *God hath made me to laugh, so that all that hear will laugh with me.*

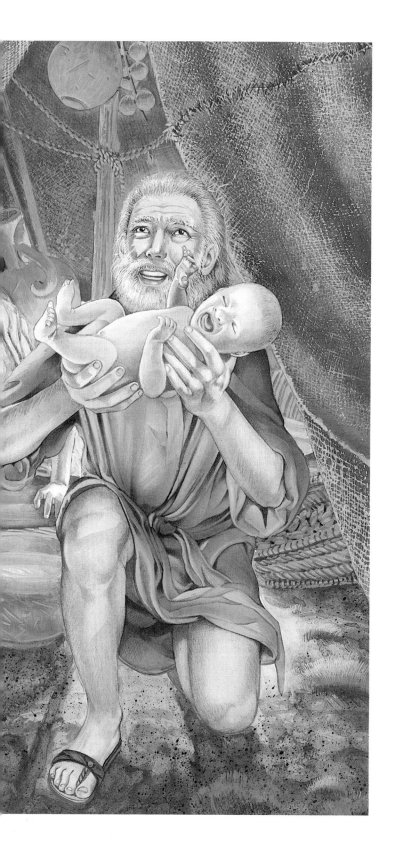

Ishmaël

The son of Abraham and his servant Hagar. Ishmael's name means : "*God hears*", and he is considered to be the ancestor of the Arabs.

Descendants

Abraham's offspring consists of far more than just the family which he fathered. His human and spiritual seed was to be as numerous as the stars in the sky.

Isaac

The son of Abraham and his wife Sarah. This child was a special miracle, for his mother Sarah was barren and of advanced age. His name means "*laughter*". Indeed his belated birth made his mother smile. He was to be the father of Jacob, the ancestor of the twelve tribes of Israel.

Countless children

A personal call

God called Abraham by his name, as one calls a beloved child who is more precious than everything else. Today, God knows the name of each of His children. He loves each person, and desires that they love and obey Him.

Promise

Through Abraham God made a promise to all nations. To His children He promises: I will love you everlastingly. I will watch over you. I will never abandon you. Nothing will ever be able to break this promise. When God promises something, it is forever!

Trust

How can one fail to trust our wise, loving and powerful God, who promises His continuous presence? Trusting God consists of believing in Him and His word, and being certain that He only seeks the very best for His children.

Doubt

Our existence is tough. Sometimes believers go through hard times. Sometimes they have the impression they are completely alone and that God has forgotten them. It is then that one must remember the promise to which God is always faithful. God was faithful to Abraham, and He is faithful to us.

Pilgrim

The believer is like a nomad. He is always on the move, a pilgrim, on the road. God calls him to progress always further, step by step, in order to grow every day a little more like His own dear son, Jesus Christ our saviour.

With Him

With Him
one is always on the road:
no question of getting bored
or settling into a routine!
With Him one is always on the
move:
no question of hanging on
to preconceived ideas
or of "every man for himself"!

With Him
there is always a great spirit
burning in one's heart:
the joyous desire
to love to the bitter end.

With Him
bread is always shared
to strengthen and uphold
those who fall by the wayside
despondent.

With Him
there is always a hand outstretched
to uplift
those who lag behind without hope
and lead them to the door
of the wedding feast opened
to all.

With Him
it is bliss!

CHAPTER 3

The son whom you love, Isaac

Jacques Le Grant:
"The Book of good manners",
Sacrifice of Abraham
(ms 297/1338 fol 35)
fifteenth century.

Onmunement some est endin
a maintenir la vie la quelleen
sa iennese il a maintenu. Si
se deuuent les iennes aduiser et mettir paine dac
queuir vertuz a celle fin que bien faire soit pla
isent au pou ᵗ preces de leur vie. Car come

Human sacrifices

Corn harvest in Roumania

In the time of Abraham the people of Canaan made human sacrifices. They believed that they would thus win the favor of their gods, good harvests and protection against their enemies. Abraham was certainly aware of these practices. As a new arrival in the land, perhaps he was invited to make towards his own God the horrible gesture of the Canaanites who offered up their children as a sacrifice. Yet he did not do it.

God does not want this

Imagine Abraham's shock when God asked him to sacrifice Isaac, the son which God had promised. This was unlike the God which Abraham followed. Yet Abraham was obedient, and in faith obeyed God's command. He didn't understand, but he was faithful.

God did not want Abraham to sacrifice his son Isaac. He wanted to test Abraham's faith. Would Abraham fully obey God? Was Abraham's faith strong enough to follow God's difficult commands? Yes it was, and because Abraham was fully faithful, God was able to fully bless him.

But there's more. This touching story is a beautiful picture of how God sacrificed His only begotten son for our sins. The death of Jesus Christ on the cross paid the penalty for our sins, and healed the broken relationship between God and His sinful creation. Just as the ram was slain as a substitute for Isaac, so Jesus was slain as our substitute. And just as Isaac *"lived again"* after the sacrifice, so Jesus rose again from the dead in victory over sin and death, offering us eternal life.

Hittite figure presenting a sheaf of wheat as an offering. Sculpture from Ivriz in Turkey

* According to the Bible, in the eighth century B.C., the king of Judah Ahaz "passed his son through fire" (2 Kings 16:3). That meant that he offered him up as a sacrifice to a foreign god. He thought that by doing this he would obtain this god's protection against the enemies who were threatening Jerusalem.

** The Bible severely condemns these sacrifices of children offered to a divinity called "Molech": "Any son of Israel or any foreigner living in Israel must be put to death if he sacrificed any of his children to Molech. The people of the community were to stone him..." (Leviticus 20:2).

Statue by Gustav Vigeland in Oslo, Norway

15

The sacrifice of Isaac

Genesis Chapter 22, verses 1-17.

And it came to pass after these things, that God did tempt Abraham, and said unto him, *Abraham*: and he said, *Behold, here I am*. And he said, *Take now **thy son,** thine only son Isaac, whom thou lovest, and get thee into the land of **Moriah**; and offer him there a **burnt** offering upon one of the mountains which I will tell thee of.* And Abraham rose up early in the morning, and saddled his ass, and took two of his young men with him, and Isaac his son, and clave the wood for the burnt offering, and rose up, and went unto the place of which God had told him. Then on the third day Abraham lifted up his eyes, and saw the place afar off. And Abraham said unto his young men, *Abide ye here with the ass; and I and the lad will go yonder and worship, and come again to you,* And Abraham took the wood of the burnt offering, and laid it upon Isaac his son; and he took the fire in his hand, and a knife; and they went both of them together. And Isaac spake unto Abraham his father, and said, *My father*: and he said, *Here am I, my son*. And he said, *Behold the fire and the wood: but where is the lamb for a burnt offering?* And Abraham said, *My son, God will provide himself a lamb for a burnt offering*: so they went both of them together. And they came to the place which God had told him of; and Abraham built an altar there, and laid the wood in order, and bound Isaac his son, and laid him on the altar upon the wood. And Abraham stretched forth is hand, and took the knife to slay his son. And the angel of the Lord called unto him out of heaven, and said, *Abraham, Abraham*: and he said, *Here am I*. And he said, *Lay not thine hand upon the lad, neither do thou any thing unto him: for now I know that thou fearest God, seeing thou hast not withheld thy son, thine only son from me.* And Abraham lifted up his eyes, and looked, and behold behind him a ram caught in a thicket by his horns: and Abraham went and took the ram, and offered him for a burnt offering in the stead of his son. And Abraham called the name of that place Jehovah-jireh: as it is said to this day, In the mount of the Lord it shall be seen. And the angel of the Lord called Abraham out of heaven the second time, And said, *By myself have I sworn, saith the Lord, for because thou hast done this thing, and hast not withheld thy son, thine only son: That in blessing I will bless thee, and in multiplying I will multiply thy seed as the stars of the heaven, and as the sand which is upon the sea shore; and thy seed shall possess the gate of his enemies . . .*

Your son

Abraham clearly loved his son, Isaac. This is clear from the many times the word "son" is repeated in the text. Try to count how many times. Can you imagine how difficult it would be for a father to sacrifice his son? How difficult was it for God to sacrifice His only son, Jesus Christ?

Moriah

We do not know for sure where the land of Moriah was. Later on, the Temple of God in Jerusalem was built, on the hill called "mount Moriah". (2 Chronicles 3;1).

Burnt Offering

The burnt offering was a sacrifice in which the animal was completely burned. It was believed that the smoke which rose up into the sky carried the offering to God. The word "holocaust" comes from this Hebrew verb 'alah which means "rise up".

God is for life

Illusion

Some people wrongly think that in order to please God one must suffer or cut themselves or even die. This is not the way God describes Himself in the Bible! How can they represent the God of love who created us and died for us as one who also requires our blood and pain?

God of love

God calls people not in order to overwhelm us with His power or with impossible requests but in order to give each one of us His love in abundance. He does not demand any great deed in return. He does ask us to respond to Him in love, to follow Him, and obey His commands.

God of goodness

God is a God of "goodness" and mercy. He desires the very best for His children. Even when we are sick or are harmed by others, He uses it for good in our lives. He would never ask us to suffer needlessly.

Sacrifice

The Bible says that "Greater love hath no man than this, that a man lay down his life for his friends." (John 15:13). When we love someone, we are willing to sacrifice everything for that person, even, if necessary, our life. Thankfully, this is seldom necessary, but aren't you thankful that God sacrificed His son because He loved us so much?

God of life

God is on the side of life. In fact, He is the Creator of life. He never demands that those who trust Him die in order to prove their faith in Him. God is a living God who gives the breath of life to all His children. Many of His children have been killed by those who are enemies of God, but their eternal life with God will never end. How much better to extend God's love and goodness to those we meet.

Search

A long time ago
they set off
to follow God
who was calling them by their name.
For a long time they have been trying
to recognize His face
and discover the places
where He is invisibly present.

So that they not lose their way,
and in order to guide their search
God has regularly left
signs for them on the way.

On their path he put
men and women
who reminded them constantly
that God prefers
a heart filled with love
to all forms of sacrifice
and to the gold of all the altars.

He sent Jesus his Son
to them
so that through
His words and gestures
they might touch
and hear God
and see His Face
of infinite tenderness.

CHAPTER • 4

Jacob the struggler

Copied in the style of **Jacopo da Ponte** known as **Bassano** (circa 1510-1592), Esau selling his birthright.

© Giraudon - Musée des Beaux-Arts, Caen (France)

Life was hard

Herd of camels with their owner in Judea

The life of the nomads was not always easy. The sun was scorching, water scarce, pastures sparse. There were often conflicts between individuals and tribes.

Abraham's descendances who lived in the land of Canaan had kept in touch with the members of their family who had stayed in Haran. Abraham had even arranged for Isaac to marry Rebecca, the daughter of his uncle Nahor.

A colorful narrative

In time, Isaac and Rebecca had twin sons ; Esau *"the hairy one "*, the first-born, and Jacob *"the supplanter "*. Esau was his father's favorite. Jacob was cherished by his mother Rebecca. The Bible explains how God intended the spiritual blessing to go to Jacob but how, in his old age, Isaac intended to give the blessing to Esau, a sinful man. But Jacob greatly desired the godly heritage and bought the birthright from Esau in exchange for a plate of lentils. Then, with the help of his mother he tricked his old blind father to gain the blessing, wrongly intended for Esau. Threatened by his brother, Jacob, took refuge in the home of his uncle Laban in Haran. He bargained with his uncle in order to obtain his daughter Rachel's hand in marriage. After more than 14 years he escaped with his family and flocks. He returned to the land of Canaan where he feared a confrontation with his brother Esau.

The Bible text (p. 22) explains to us how the *"supplanter "* becomes *"Israel"**, that is *"he who struggled victoriously with God"*.

* **"Israel"** *is not only Jacob's new name. It is also the name of the people which was to come from him. His twelve sons were the fathers of the twelve tribes of Israel. Thus, the members of God's chosen people are called "sons of Israel". Their life was and is often a struggle. But just as the mysterious experiences of their father were victorious, so God has enabled them to overcome great struggles.*

Young peasant girl in Syria

Jacob struggles with God

Genesis Chapter 32 : 22-31.

And he rose up that night, and took his two wives, and his two wom-enservants, and his **eleven sons**, and passed over the ford Jabbok. And he took them, and sent them over the brook, and sent over that he had. And Jacob was left **alone** ; and there wrestled a man with him until the breaking of the day. And when he saw that he prevailed not against him, he touched the hollow of his thigh ; and the hollow of Jacob's thigh was out of joint, as he wrestled with him. And he said, *Let me go, for the day breaketh.* And he said, *I will not let thee go, except thou bless me.* And he said unto him, *What [is] thy name ?* And he said, *Jacob.* And he said, *Thy name shall be called no more Jacob, but Israel : for as a prince hast thou power with God and with men, and hast prevailed.*

And Jacob asked [him], and said, *Tell [me], I pray thee, thy name.* And he said, *Wherefore [is] it [that] thou dost ask after my name ?* And he blessed him there. And Jacob called the name of the place Peniel : *for I have seen God face to face, and my life is* **preserved**. And as he passed over Penuel the sun rose upon him, and he halted upon his thigh.

Eleven children

Jacob's twelfth son, Benjamin, was not yet born when the family returned to Canaan.

Alone

The Bible speaks of two lonely experiences of Jacob. The first when he leaves for Haran (Genesis 32 : 10-22), the second when he comes back from Haran (text opposite). In the first he discovers that God would never leave him. In the second God granted him His blessing as a result of Jacob's prevailing prayer.

His life was spared

At that time it was believed that one could not see God and live. However, at times God appeared to men with a special message.

Apprenticeship

Alone

It is up to each person to decide alone, in his or her own soul and conscience, to fol-low God. Nobody can do it for us. We can receive support or advice but it is up to each of us to choose the way of salvation, love, faith, and gift of self . . .

Struggle

Life as a human being and as a child of God is a daily struggle. Indeed it consists of resisting the temptations which attempt to entrap each of us in sin. It consists of choosing right over wrong and good over evil in our thoughts and actions.

Place

Some think that each of us has to work courageously to find his or her place in the community, in the family, amongst friends, in the world . . . ! In order for people to listen do we not have to make ourselves heard? In order to be loved do we not have to go out to others and make ourselves known? In order to achieve something do we not have to join up with others and put our personal capacities at their disposal?

Status

Some people, for fear of being rejected or unloved tell tales in order to impress others, or else they try to show off, push oth-ers aside and even take their place . . . To achieve this they don't hesitate to lie. In reality it is themselves that they are de-luding!

Ladder

Our human experience often seems like a ladder which is breathtakingly high and uneven and has to be scaled with the utmost caution. Yet our saviour has promised never to leave us. With His help, we can scale even the tallest ladder.

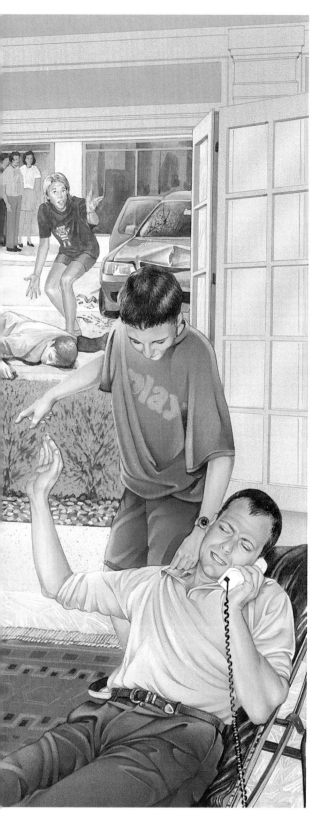

What a struggle

What a struggle with God
every day!

We are so comfortable
in the soft cocoon of sloth
which is content with making the least
effort possible.
And God comes to shake up our torpor
and remind us of all the variety
of talents that he has sown in us
like seeds
to be nurtured in view of the harvest!

We are so comfortable
with the little falsehoods that mask
our refusal to love. And God comes
to speak to us of love
to be given out without counting the cost!

We are so comfortable
with our petty revenge
and our poisonous jealousy.
And He comes to urge us to forgive
and pray for our enemies.

What a struggle with God!
He leaves us no peace!
He comes to spur us on
to live every day
even more generously
ever more transparently,
ever more humanly:
like beloved children!

CHAPTER 5

The saga of Joseph

Diego Velazquez Rodrigez de Silva (1599-1660), The bloodied tunic of Joseph brought back to Jacob.

© Giraudon - Monastère de l'Escurial (Espagne)

In Egypt

Jordanian nomads in their tent home

Abraham's descendants were nomads. They moved around a great deal. They were often in contact with Egypt* and caravan tradesmen who took their goods to Egypt. The story of Joseph's slavery and rise to power in Egypt has been recognized as one of the best ever written. Through times of great tribulation and temptation. Joseph remains faithful to God, and God blesses him, and uses him as the means to preserve the people of Israel.

Pyramid of Giza in Egypt

A real storybook

The Bible portrays Joseph as an intelligent, wise** and exemplary man. He lets God guide him in the difficulties of daily life. In the story of Joseph, in contrast to those of Abraham, Isaac and Jacob, there is never a mention of an exceptional intervention of God***. Joseph uses the abilities God has given him, and God blessed him. Today, God guides us in daily life, just as he guided Joseph. These pages (Genesis 37 to 50) read like a real story book.

Palestinian camp in Judea

* **The Egyptians** in Joseph's day were powerful, well-educated and wealthy. Their building projects have hardly been matched by modern technology.

** The Bible instructs us all to gain wisdom. Joseph is portrayed as an ideal "wise-man". He bears his lot patiently. He does not let himself be seduced. He knows when to speak and when to keep silent. He counsels the king, but remains unpretentious.

*** In the story of Joseph there are no visions or mysterious voices, no appearances made by God or an Angel of God.

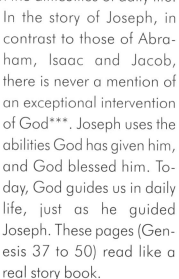

Joseph is sold by his brothers

Genesis 50 : 18-20.

Here is a summary of the story of Joseph:

Jacob had twelve sons. Joseph, the son of Rachel, was his father's favorite, and his brothers were jealous. They decided to sell him to a caravan which was traveling to Egypt. They soaked his tunic in goat's blood, and brought it back to their father, leading Jacob to believe that his son had been killed by a wild beast.

In Egypt Joseph was bought by Potiphar, the captain of the guard. Soon, Joseph became the head of his house. But the Egyptian's wife made romantic advances to him which he refused. Unjustly accused, Joseph was imprisoned with two of the Pharaoh's servants, the chief baker and the chief cup-bearer. Each of them had a **dream**. Joseph explained their meaning, the cup bearer was to be freed and the baker executed, which soon happened. One day, the Pharaoh had a dream that none of his wise men were able to explain. The cup bearer then remembered Joseph. The Pharaoh had him brought out of prison and Joseph deciphered his double dream: seven sleek and fat cows and seven ugly and thin cows; seven healthy and full ears of wheat then seven withered and scorched ones. Joseph explained: *"There will be seven years of plenty, then seven years of **famine**. You must start preparing for them right now."* The Pharaoh put Joseph as the second in charge in the whole of Egypt. During the years of plenty he had the grain put into storage, and during the years of famine, Joseph sold it. Since there was also a famine in Palestine Jacob twice sent his sons to buy wheat in Egypt. Joseph recognized them without revealing his identity. He put them to the test several times in order to bring them to admit their guilt and to test the sincerity of their repentance. He finally revealed to them that he was their brother. They were filled with joy and fear and asked forgiveness. Then Pharaoh invited Jacob and his whole family to come and settle in Egypt. Their descendances remained there for several centuries until the time of Moses.

The Bible itself gives the key to the saga of Joseph: God brings a greater good out of evil.

> ... **His brothers then came and threw themselves down before him:**
>
> *"We are your slaves,"* **they said. But Joseph said to them,** *"Don't be afraid. Am I in the place of God? You intended to harm me, but God intended it for the good in order to save many lives."*

Dream

Dreams have always intrigued human beings. What is the origin of the scenes that we see when we dream? Usually they have no meaning, but in antiquity it was believed that God spoke to men through dreams. The wisemen of Pharaoh claimed they could interpret dreams, but only Joseph, with God's help, was able to interpret Pharaoh's strange dream.

Famine

This calamity occurred frequently in antiquity. In Canaan it was mostly caused by lack of rain or by parasites which killed the crops. In Egypt it was usually the result of the irregular flooding of the Nile River.

Dignity

Jealousy

Why are people jealous, as if others' success wounded them, or as it other's beauty were unbearable to them, or as if other's talents overshadowed their own gifts? Jealousy is a terrible evil. It can not accept that another person be great or praiseworthy or happy or blessed of God.

Evil Desires

Because of jealousy and envy, evil desires may take possession of a person's mind and heart. Their own sin leads them to wrong choices. Then in a hidden or roundabout way they seek to undermine people's happiness or honor or even do them harm.

Sale

Sometimes people sell their brothers and sisters, their neighbors. Selling one's neighbor can consist of hurting him or her, wounding with mocking words or words of hate, or even with physical blows, exposing him or her to spitefulness and calamity, attacking their reputation. Selling one's neighbor is the moral equivalent of murder!

Dream

Who does not dream of being great and working wonders? Who does not dream of making the earth more beautiful with new inventions and discoveries? Dreaming is a capacity which God has given to every human being. Yet dreams are not enough! Often one has to work hard to make dreams come true.

Happiness

It is terrible to be without food or work. Another sort of famine exists, sometimes far more agonizing than the lack of bread. This famine has devastating effects in many people. It consists of being deprived of dignity and respect, deprived of the warm and friendly presence of others' love. As children of God we can extend His love to those in need.

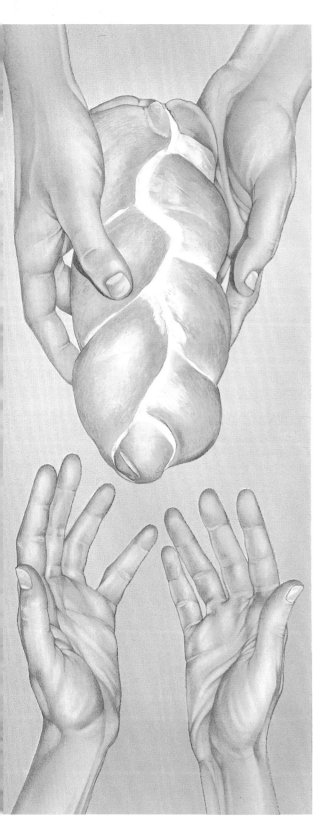

He, on the contrary

The wicked
may sell their neighbor
to mockery and subject him or her
to their sneering spite.
He, God,
laughs at no-one.
He, on the contrary,
always comes to the defense
of His children on earth.

The wicked
may sharpen
their rancorous tongue
on their neighbors' backs
and tear them apart with their jealous claws.
He, God,
never wounds anyone.
He, on the contrary, always rejoices
at the success and the pleasure
of all His children on earth.

He, God,
never leaves
a single one of His children on earth
without consolation.
To all of them,
like daily bread,
He gives every day
His nourishing
tenderness!

Your family

You know your brothers and sisters, your parents, your grand-parents, aunts and uncles and cousins. You can discover the names of your great-grand-parents and of other members of your family.

Your family tree

Using all your discoveries you can begin to draw up your family tree.

Usually one designates :

men by the sign of the planet Mars : ♂

and women by sign of the planet Venus : ♀

As a start, note down what you already know and fill in the gaps little by little.

Here as an example is Nicholas' family tree :

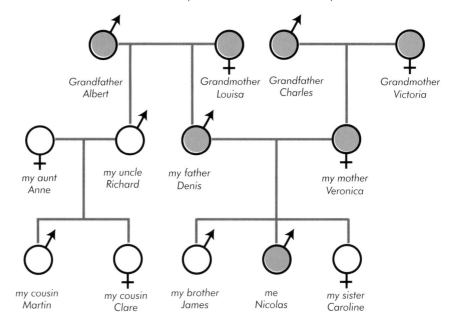

Grandfather Albert — Grandmother Louisa — Grandfather Charles — Grandmother Victoria

my aunt Anne — my uncle Richard — my father Denis — my mother Veronica

my cousin Martin — my cousin Clare — my brother James — me Nicolas — my sister Caroline

You are not alone

It is interesting to write down the year of birth of the members of your family and find out from which region or country they come. Thus you will discover your roots. You are part of a family and all the families are part of the great human family.

Abraham's family

In Abraham's time, 4000 years ago, nobody had identity papers or family record books. Each person indicated his or her identity using the name of his or her ancestors, Thus Joseph called himself :
" Joseph, son of Jacob, son of Isaac, son of Abraham ".

Joseph's ancestry

The story of Joseph and his ancestors has been told in this book.
So you can now draw up his family tree.

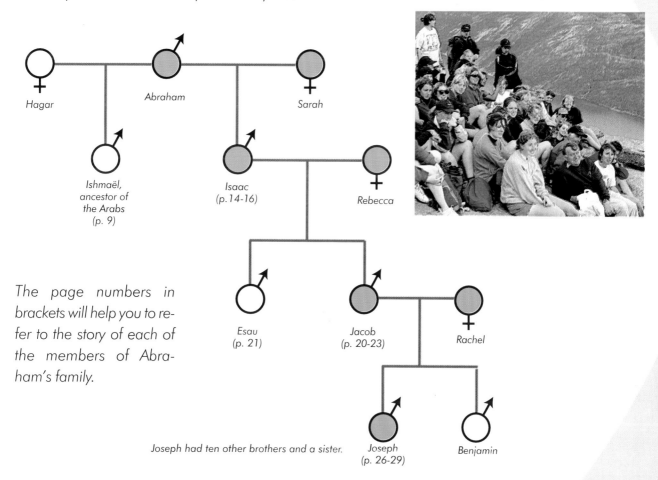

Hagar

Abraham

Sarah

Ishmaël,
ancestor of
the Arabs
(p. 9)

Isaac
(p.14-16)

Rebecca

The page numbers in brackets will help you to refer to the story of each of the members of Abraham's family.

Esau
(p. 21)

Jacob
(p. 20-23)

Rachel

Joseph had ten other brothers and a sister.

Joseph
(p. 26-29)

Benjamin

All the families

God chose Abraham and his family.
Through him God blessed *"all the families on the earth "*; nobody is excluded from the vast human family nor from the love of God.

A Final Note :

Faith. It's a short word that sometimes takes a long time to understand. But this is a story of a man who believed God and inspire all of us to find out just what faith really is.

Imagine leaving the only home you've ever known and settling in a strange place. The familiar sights and sounds of the city give way to a desolate and dusty road pointing dimly to a new life. Then imagine being told to kill the child you love more than your own life. What would you do?

Abraham experienced all this and more. He walked through his own amazing history because he believed God.

You see, God has a plan for each of us. He know everything and sees both the beginning and the end. He knew Abraham would be blessed if he simply believed – if he simply had faith in what God wanted accomplished. Abraham was never able to count all his blessings . . . but they came to him because he first believed God.

The awesome story of Abraham's life of faith is told here with amazing detail. Come see why Abraham is called the first man of faith.

An Awesome Adventure Titles Now Available:

· Jesus the Child
· Jesus Is Calling
· The Creation
· Abraham's Family

Upcoming Titles Available Soon:

· Jesus Heals
· Who Is Jesus
· Moses
· The Promised Land

The migration of Abraham's family along the fertile Crescent

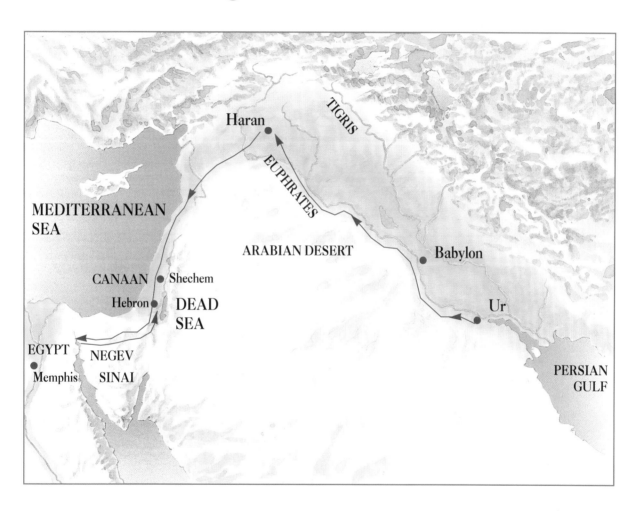

Abraham's family

Edited by
John D. Morris

TEXT

Albert HARI - Charles SINGER

PICTURE RESEARCH

Sandrine WINTER

PHOTOGRAPHY

Frantisek ZVARDON

Gabriel LOISON

Patrice THÉBAULT

LAYOUT

Studio BAYLE

ILLUSTRATIONS

Mariano VALSESIA

Betti FERRERO

MIA. Milan Illustrations Agency

FIRST PRINTING: JUNE 1998

Copyright © 1998 by Master Books
for the CBA U.S. edition.

For information write: Master Books, P.O. Box 727, Green Forest, AR 72638.

ISBN: 0-89051-243-4

© ÉDITIONS DU SIGNE 1997